VICTIM OF BULLYING

Before taking his life a boy wrote a message ... the class diary, a portion of which I quote.

"I decided to kill myself because day after day I go to school and only bad things happen. Nothing good ever happens to me. If the kids in my class could be in my shoes they would understand how I feel. If only they knew how I feel every day. Even in my dreams there are nothing but bad things.

The only one I can talk to is the hamster, but the hamster can't speak back. Maybe my being born was a mistake···. I can't stop the tears now. There was one, only one thing I wanted while I was alive, a friend I could talk to, really talk to from the heart. Just one friend like that, only one, was all I wanted."

07/03/04

The Bystander

I knew you when you stood up tall and looked the world in the eye.
I remember the smile and the way you laughed
But that's gone now, by and by.

You seem to have got much smaller turned inside yourself
somewhere.
They have dragged you down, robbed your self esteem
And they didn't seem to care.

You were an easy target you didn't put up a fight.
Your humiliation was the source of power
Which they flexed with all their might.

Their bullying was like an addiction, needing to be fed.
So I now confess I felt relief
When they picked on you instead

So I stood by and watched them, I didn't say a word.
As they picked at you like vultures
Feasting on some tiny bird.

You must have known I'd abandoned you, felt lost, lonely and
afraid.
I wish now I had done something.
I cry for the difference I could have made.

The No Blame Approach

Michael is being bullied...

A support group method

Barbara Maines
George Robinson

Lucky Duck is more than a publishing house and training agency. George Robinson and Barbara Maines founded the company in the 1980s when they worked together as a head and psychologist developing innovative strategies to support challenging students.

They have an international reputation for their work on bullying, self-esteem, emotional literacy and many other subjects of interest to the world of education.

George and Barbara have set up a regular news-spot on the website. Twice yearly these items will be printed as a newsletter. If you would like to go on the mailing list to receive this then please contact us:

e-mail newsletter@luckyduck.co.uk   website www.luckyduck.co.uk

ISBN: 1 873 942 40 0

Published by Lucky Duck Publishing Ltd.

www.luckyduck.co.uk

Printed in the UK by Antony Rowe Ltd

Thank you to our actors:

Michael, Joseph, Marlon, Oscar, Tommy, Conrad,

our voices:

Polly, Kate, Alex, Megan, Henry, Emily,

and especially to Jane Sleigh, the teacher and Lee Cox, the producer for their brilliant work on this project.

At primary school things were fine

At secondary school they are just not fine

All my best friends have turned bad

They bully me and make me sad

I don't want to break friends

      because they <u>were</u> nice

      but I want to be with them

      but how can I

When they bully me?

Graham Hunter

Contents

Michael's been bullied
- a peer support group method

The No Blame Approach

Introduction

All schools have a responsibility to reduce bullying. In many the school rules will include a reference to the requirement that:

▸ every member of the school behaves in a considerate way and respects the rights of others.

In tutorial and curriculum approaches these aspects of individual and group relationships may be explored and students can be encouraged to approach adults for help when things go wrong for them or their peers.

In this way schools can demonstrate to pupils, parents and carers that bullying is a serious problem and that, when witnessed or reported, it will be 'seen and listened to and that something will be done to make things better.'

In our first publication on the subject, 'Stamp out Bullying,' we explain a preventive approach and refer to other interventions such as pastoral work, drama, classroom charters and other school based initiatives.

These are preventive interventions, intended to create a safer climate and reduce school bullying.

BUT...

there will always be some bullying - this is a 'normal' part of school life and however undesirable it needs to be recognised as such.

In this publication we go on to discuss our 'reactive' approach; - a step-by-step plan to support teachers when bullying has happened.

In this work book which accompanies the video of Michael's story we will:

▸ question the effectiveness of strategies often used in schools

▸ explain our no blame approach

▸ provide a series of readings and activities to support your learning.

How to use the package

As we introduce our ideas in this book we will be asking you to think about the ways in which bullying is dealt with in your establishment and whether the alternatives suggested in here; 'the no blame approach,' might be adopted as an alternative.

In order to give staff an opportunity to think and discuss we are suggesting some activities as well as reading and watching the video. The materials could be adapted for a whole day's in-service or presented at a shorter workshop or as a series of staff meetings.

We would advise that you work through activities 1 - 9 before watching the video material.

Photocopy pages for use in your own establishment. Extra copies can be obtained in bulk for inset days. Please enquire from Lucky Duck Publishing.

Activity one

Why don't you...

begin by agreeing what you mean by the word bullying? Talk to the person next to you and try to tease out the real meaning of this word.

How might you define the terms

'bully'	**'victim'**

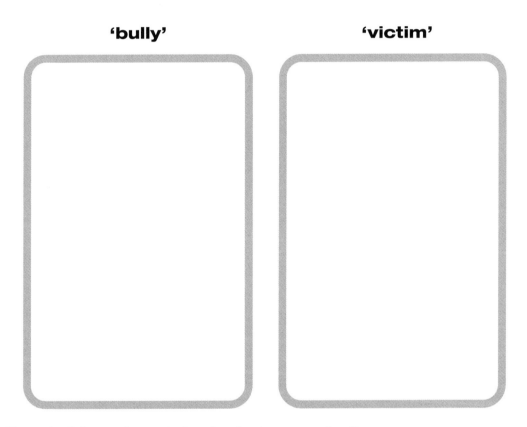

Does bullying refer only to physical aggression?

What other acts are considered to be bullying?

Who bullies whom?

How common is it?

Does the term apply only to one-off incidents of nastiness?

When you have discussed your own ideas you may want to turn to Appendix one to read some of our views and some of the research information.

Activity two

How do you know it is happening?

There are only two ways that we are likely to learn that bullying has happened and we rely on:

▸ what we see and hear

▸ what we are told.

Discuss in a group all the ways in which incidents of bullying might come to the attention of members of staff.

In what ways might they be hidden from you?

What can you do to find out more? Use lots of different school environments to discover your answers. You might like to refer to some ideas in Appendix two at this point.

Activity three

How do you deal with it at present?

Do you sometimes take no action at all?

If so what is your fear?

- ▸ that you might make things worse

- ▸ that you don't know what to do for the best.

Do you think this is sometimes a matter for students to sort out and not the responsibility of teachers?

Read the following two scenarios and plan how you would deal with them.

[Both are descriptions of scenes taken from the Central TV programme 'Sticks and Stones.']

Pauline

You observe a group of four girls in the corner of the room. Danielle and Yasmin seem to be laughing a lot and maybe making fun of Pauline who is the only one standing. Charlotte looks on. You overhear the conversation and it is about parties and clothes. All three seem to be making fun of Pauline but although she looks a bit awkward and sad she does say that she is going to the party as well and she seems to join in the chatter.

What might you do? Devise and action plan.

Kathleen

Kathleen and Stefan are walking along the path when Claire, Ramon and Nadine run into them. The group stops and Ramon approaches Kathleen, takes her coke can away and demands that Kathleen apologise on her knees. Claire backs up Ramon's sneering and domineering behaviour. Kathleen complies silently. Ramon spits into the coke can. Nadine comments that this is not right but Ramon defiantly repeats the spitting. At this point Stefan looks very upset and says that he cannot take this - he is going to get help. The adult intervention starts at the point when Stefan knocks on the staffroom door and tells what is happening. This scene has not been observed by any adult.

What might you do? Devise and action plan.

Activity four
Reading

The challenge to school practice

Many of the strategies we use may be ineffective in changing the behaviour of the bully. We approach the situation with strong feelings of anger and frustration towards the bully and sympathy for the victim. We have a responsibility to the students and their parents or carers to respond effectively and the measure of the success of our intervention has to be the degree to which it stops the bullying. Some of the responses often made by teachers are not successful in achieving this and we discuss them below. Please try and set aside any feelings of retribution towards the bully - your aim is not justice or morality; it is to change behaviour and thus achieve the best outcome for the victim.

Dangers of labelling

Although we use the terms 'bully' and 'victim' in this and other publications we do not think it is helpful to use them as labels in school. We know that to call a young person by any name must affect her self-image and must be difficult for parents or carers to accept when we want to work co-operatively with them.

Getting to the bottom of it

It seems common sense to question students about facts and reasons when bad behaviour is brought to our attention. When we talk to the young people they often report that they give teachers the answers they want - that will get them out of the room as soon as possible.

When you question young people about the facts they will give their own perspective and these are often contradictory, especially when a bully is trying to extract herself from blame. You may then be distracted from effective action in your quest for the truth.

Even less helpful is to ask students to explain why they behave in a certain way. It is very hard to explain our actions, maybe impossible in a way which will satisfy a teacher. We were recently told about a small pupil who undid the safety bolts on a climbing frame and his teacher asked him why he had done it. His predictable reply was, "Don't know, Miss." The teacher became frustrated and we asked her why she thought he had done it. "Because he is disturbed and attention seeking," she replied. Was the teacher really expecting the boy to reply..."Well, Miss, it is because I am disturbed"?

Changing the victim

Over and over again we hear from victims that they are advised and urged to change their behaviour in some way, either by parents, carers, teachers or through group work. They try to 'stand up for themselves,' 'hit back,' 'walk away,' 'pretend you don't care,' and each time their failure to act in a way which ends their misery just makes it worse. They feel it is their own fault that this is happening to them. It is not. Whatever their own inadequacy or difficulty, it is not their fault and it is not their responsibility to stop it. It is our responsibility and we must give them that message loud and clear if we are not to compound their unhappiness.

There is nothing wrong with assertiveness training for everyone. There is plenty of benefit to be gained from social skills programmes for lots of students who are having difficulties in making relationships. However, these interventions should not be linked directly with the victim's plight but with more general developmental work.

Punishment

Maybe the biggest challenge for us is to advise you to abandon punishment as a response to the bullies. We take a pragmatic approach and suggest that punishment simply does not work; in fact it will often make things worse when the bully takes further revenge on the victim.

If you want to encourage disclosure and you want to work positively with bullies then everyone in school must know that effective action will be taken but that it will not lead to punishment. We cannot agree with the following views.

In "Bullying - a practical guide to coping for schools," Eric Jones (1991) writes,

"Punish bullies. Record punishment and the reasons for it. Show him what you are putting on file and make him pay for whatever time it cost you to sort it out."

page 23.

and in another chapter John Pearce (1991) advises that when a bully is caught in the act we should respond by,

"Telling a bully that he or she will be dealt with later without specifying how or when can be very effective. The bully is likely to worry about what may happen..."

page 84.

Bullying is an antisocial behaviour resorted to by inadequate people and we must respond in a way which will be helpful to their learning of improved behaviour. Increasing their anxiety and alienation from us is not likely to work!

Activity five
Reading

– this section may be copied for every participant.

What doesn't work...YOU WILL NOT DO THIS!

Paul had arrived in the first year with a reputation for being difficult. He had poor relationships with peers and was an obvious scapegoat. He was later described by the educational psychologist as a 'blob'. In spite of being in a class who did not know him previously he was very soon the victim of verbal bullying, much of which he provoked himself and much of which he enjoyed as a form of attention which he failed to get in any other way.

Whether this would have reached its own conclusion is difficult to say because when it reached its peak his class group was changed and he was given the opportunity to start again with a new set of peers. In the second year it began again. This time the form teacher could bear it no longer. The deputy head in charge of lower school talked to the class and to the particular group who were most guilty of the verbal bullying, demanding that this should stop, that they had no right to bully whatever the reason and that they would be punished because the school did not accept bullying. He explained that whatever Paul did there was no reason to treat him in this way. 'This way' included teasing - about physique, ability, setting him up - taking pens, pencils from others and putting them in his bag, enticing him to break minor rules and then telling on him, hiding his property and name-calling.

The group and whole class resented the attention Paul got from this, but failed to see that they were actually causing the increased attention. They resented being punished for trying to 'put Paul in his place' and although the verbal bullying (within teachers' earshot) stopped, the bullying became far more subversive and physical. Paul was actually bruised and too frightened to tell anyone. He was subjected to threats and the physical bullying was continued out of school. Paul became more introverted and his behaviour far more antisocial. Bear in mind that many of his peers had actually tired of the early bullying before the deputy head had threatened action.

Now in his fourth year Paul still has difficulty with peer relationships. He has again changed class groups. A considerable amount of counselling has taken place with Paul which has failed to help him to change the way he feels about himself and his behaviour because of negative feedback from others. He is still set up, he is still called names and recently he retaliated and broke a bone in his hand in doing so. His relationships are better with a small number of pupils with whom he worked in a small group and who also have some difficulty in relating to others. They could understand Paul's feelings because theirs were similar and in small group work some empathy was generated.

Generally, however, the bullying continues and Paul is a very unhappy, antisocial boy.

Comment

A process which fails to engage the bully and makes no attempt to enhance feelings of concern and understanding is unlikely to bring about any fundamental change in behaviour.

Maines & Robinson 1991 page 17

Activity six

Why don't you...

reconsider your plans for Pauline and Kathleen and discuss;

Did you include:-

- ▸ doing nothing?
- ▸ labelling the bully and victim?
- ▸ getting to the bottom of it?
- ▸ changing the victim?
- ▸ punishment?

Did you do more to help Kathleen than Pauline?

Do you wish to make any modifications to your plan?

Modified action plans for:

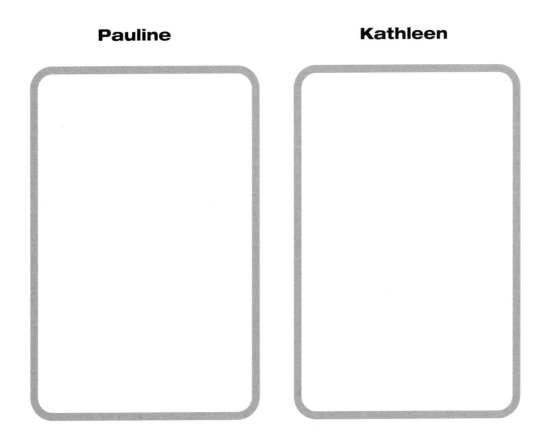

Pauline

Kathleen

[You may not yet be sure what you want to put in its place but do not hesitate to strike out any actions which now seem to be of little value or even make things worse.]

Activity seven
Reading

– this section may be copied for every participant.

Because we all have such strong reactions of anger, distress and even revenge when we encounter bullying, it is hard to take a clear view of the 'normality' of the behaviour. To say something is normal means that it frequently occurs even when there is no pathological deviance. This does not mean it is desirable.

Read the page below and discuss your reactions in small groups.

Bullying is 'normal'

Many of those reading this publication will have had some close relationship with a very young baby at some time in their lives and they will remember the self-centred and relentlessly demanding behaviour exhibited by a tiny, dependent human being. If babies were big and parents small then parents would undoubtedly be bullied! You may also remember if you are a parent or carer or have had close relationships with young children, the first time that the child was upset or cried, not because some need or demand was unmet, but because of a sadness or hurt felt on behalf of another person or creature. This emergence of 'empathy' is a complex step in social and emotional development and it is upon these feelings that kind and unselfish behaviours are based.

We believe that it is not helpful to regard bullying as abnormal or evil. Many of us will remember standing back and at least colluding with, if not participating in, some hurtful behaviour towards another person because it increased our own sense of belonging or identity that we were not the one being rejected. There are so many examples in our recent history of whole nations of people, almost without exception, standing back and allowing bullying to the point of genocide.

A willingness to step outside a peer group and stand alongside someone who is rejected and harmed takes strength and courage. It puts the 'rescuer' at risk of rejection herself and the success of her stand is likely to depend upon her social or physical status. We are likely then to take this risk only when we identify with the distress of the victim and we feel that our intervention is likely to bring about some change; when we feel involved and powerful.

Witnesses of bullying or those who care for the victims might have very strong feelings of anger and a need to punish the perpetrators. If an adult who is in a position of power uses her authority to stop the bullying then it may have a short term effect upon that particular situation but it is unlikely to change the status or identity of the bully and victim. There may well be a risk that the victim is further damaged because the bully was thwarted… "I will get you later!"

(We)…suggest that the primary focus of our plan to reduce bullying should be upon the feelings and status of the bully. She should be given the opportunity to acknowledge that there is a problem, to understand the degree of distress suffered, and to feel that her ability to change her behaviour is recognised. This can only be achieved by working directly with the young people involved.

Maines & Robinson 1991 page 6

Activity eight
Reading

– this section may be copied for every participant.

Read the account below of a way of dealing with bullying in school.

What works...THERE IS A PROBLEM; ANDREW IS FEELING BAD

The phone call from Andrew's parents requesting a meeting was not totally unexpected. I had been aware for a few months that he had an apt and rather uncomplimentary nickname and in class he seemed rather isolated. I understood from the teacher who had accompanied a group of students on a field trip that the nickname had been used frequently on that trip and that several students had been spoken to about using the nickname and upsetting Andrew.

When the meeting took place with Andrew and his parents it was apparent that he and they were very distressed. He had been taunted by the name until two o'clock in the morning on the field course, cars drove into their cul-de-sac and students called out the nickname and Andrew had also been taunted when the family was showing a visitor from abroad a local place of interest.

Andrew had wanted to return home early from the field course - only the support of another sympathetic student had kept him there - and he was considering abandoning his A-level course.

I saw Andrew on his own having first asked him to write down exactly how he felt. He told me he felt upset, unhappy and pursued in every part of his life. He had tried to ignore the name-calling but it didn't go away, it simply became more persistent. He said he, "felt like beating their heads in, like running away, unable to cope." I found out the names of the students who were the ring leaders and saw them as a group. I explained to them exactly how Andrew was feeling and that he was considering leaving school. I told them that this was a real problem for us all and we must think about what we could do about it. At this point one boy spoke up and told the group that he had also been a victim of teasing during the previous year. There seemed

17

to be a feeling of concern and I left the matter there, arranging to meet with each of the group individually a week later. When I talked to them alone I discovered that they had all apologised to Andrew and that they were also going to intervene when other students used the nickname.

Comment

By telling the bullies about Andrew's hurt and upset in a powerful but non-blameful way this tutor was able to illicit from the group an empathetic response to his distress. The group included enough kids who behave in a sociable way for this to work and the balance shifted from 'nasty' to 'nice.'

Taking the view that bullying is an interaction which establishes group identity, dominance and status at the expense of another, then it is only by the development of 'higher values' such as empathy, consideration, unselfishness, that the bully is likely to relinquish her behaviour and function differently in a social setting. If the preventive policy depends upon policing the environment, forbidding the behaviour, encouraging the victims and punishing the perpetrators then no lasting change can be expected.

Maines & Robinson 1991 page 16 & 17

Note

The bullying stopped, Andrew went on to take his exams and when he left school his parents wrote a letter of thanks to the tutor who had intervened so successfully on his behalf.

Activity nine
Reading

– this section may be copied for every participant.

Read the scenario below and discuss how you might react now that you have read Andrew's story.

John

John Jones has an attendance problem which has been getting worse recently and you have asked both parents to come into school. Mr Jones says that a group of older boys have been following John about. There has been no violence but they have a menacing presence and this is happening in and out of school. They don't stop until John shows that he is upset and runs away. Three boys are always involved and another four who sometimes join in. Mr Jones seems very sympathetic and worried that sometimes John comes home hungry saying that he has had no dinner because he lost his money. Mr Jones suspects that it is being taken off him but John denies this. Mrs Jones is less sympathetic: she feels that John should make friends with other people and just walk away from the gang. "He's got to learn to stand up for himself!"

Activity ten

Watch the video

When bullying has been observed or reported then the following steps can be taken:

Step one - meet with the victim

When the teacher finds out that bullying has happened she starts by talking to the victim about his feelings. She does not question him about the incidents but she does need to know who was involved.

Step two - convene a meeting with the people involved

The teacher arranges to meet with the group of pupils who have been involved. This will include some bystanders or colluders and even friends of the victim who joined in but did not initiate any bullying. We find that a group of six to eight young people works well.

Step three - explain the problem

She tells them about the way the victim is feeling and might use a poem, piece of writing or a drawing to emphasise his distress. At no time does she discuss the details of the incidents or allocate blame to the group.

Step four - share responsibility

The teacher does not attribute blame but states that she knows that the group are responsible and can do something about it.

Step five - ask the group for their ideas

Each member of the group is encouraged to suggest a way in which the victim could be helped to feel happier. The teacher gives some positive responses but she does not go on to extract a promise of improved behaviour.

Step six - leave it up to them

The teacher ends the meeting by passing over the responsibility to the group to solve the problem. She arranges to meet with them again individually to see how things are going.

Step seven - meet them again

About a week later the teacher discusses with each student, including the victim, how things have been going. This allows the teacher to monitor the bullying and keeps the young people involved in the process.

Every night I cry myself to sleep,
Why me?
Violently I wake up,
I had a nightmare.

Help! I cry as the figure loomed towards me,
The figure shouted, "Don't tell or there's more!"

I faked illness that morning,
Eighth time I'd done it,
Mum's getting suspicious,
Asking difficult questions.

"Where did you get those bruises?"
"Are you being bullied?"
"No!" I shout,
"There's nothing wrong."

I went to school today.
He demanded money.
I refused.
He took it anyway.

Another bruise for my collection,
And again I ask the question,
"Why me?"

by Alex Thomas

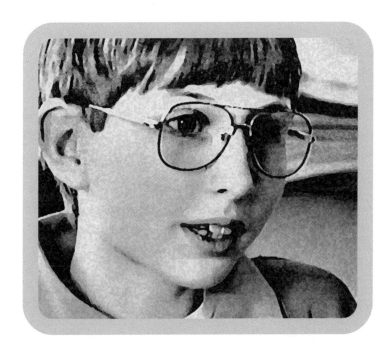

Activity eleven

Discuss Michael's story

We hope that the activities and the video have given you some real images of the ways in which interventions can be helpful. The 'no blame approach' is easy to implement, and we have had many reports of success from primary aged children through to sixth form.

If you decide to implement this as a school policy then you may wish to consider the following points:

Will everyone use this approach or will it be tried out by a few?

Is it possible to have more than one response operating in school?

How will you present it to parents and carers?

How will you record and evaluate the interventions?

Activity twelve

Plan 'no blame approach' responses for the following two scenarios.

Rosie

Rosie is a large aggressive girl, who is unkempt, her language can be very colourful and she is unpopular with her classmates. You get a report from a form tutor that informs you that Rosie has been bullying some of the members of her tutor group. She has a reputation as a bully amongst the pupils and teachers but no serious incidents have come to you before.

You ask teachers on duty to watch Rosie and to report back to you. She does play with younger pupils and can be over vigorous in her play, but it's difficult to decide if it's deliberate. What is more surprising is that it becomes obvious that Rosie's classmates deliberately exclude her and subject her to a lot of taunting

Wayne

Wayne is sent to you because he has hit Simon after a games lesson. He tells you that Simon hid his football boots before games and he could only find one, this meant he missed football. After the game Simon just happened to find it and he laughed as he gave it back. Wayne lost his temper and punched Simon in the face (there are no injuries). He is genuinely sorry and he tells you how unhappy he is because this is not an isolated incidents and a number of pupils seem to enjoy hiding his coat, pencils, rulers etc.

You know about Wayne. He is a pupil that generates little sympathy, one teacher once described him as a spoilt brat who can't look after himself because his mother indulges him. You discuss the incident with the classteacher. He agrees that sometimes the other pupils do hide Wayne's things, it's not malicious just a bit of fun and Wayne deserves all he gets because he's no angel.

24

Appendix 1

Suggested definitions for the terms 'bully' and 'victim'.

BULLY - a person or group behaving in a way which might meet needs for excitement, status, material gain or group process and does not recognise or meet the needs and rights of the other people/person who are harmed by the behaviour.

VICTIM - a person or group that is harmed by the behaviour of others and who does not have the resources, status, skill, ability, to counteract or stop the harmful behaviour.

We do not differentiate between 'bullying - by an individual' and 'mobbing - by a group' as discussed by Anatol Pikas (1989). This is because we are describing situations in which, even if the bully is operating solo, her behaviour is usually witnessed in some way by others. If the witness supports the bully, however passive that support might be, then the behaviour is in some way owned by the whole group and the strengths of the group can be encouraged in order to confront the behaviour. Where the bullying occurs in true secrecy, unknown to any witness other than the victim, then interventions are unlikely unless the behaviour is reported by the victim.

Does it refer only to physical aggression?

The definitions of bullying vary but they all are clear in that bullying is more than just physical aggression,

What other acts are considered to be bullying?

Any behaviour which harms others who do not have the skills or resources to counter this behaviour could be seen as bullying. It may be exhibited as:

▸ physical harm

▸ threat of physical harm

▸ nasty name calling or teasing

▸ extortion, demand for money or favours

▸ exclusion, deliberately leaving someone out of an activity.

We need to be aware that not all aggression is bullying, nor all name-calling. It becomes bullying when it is exercised through the use of power rather than an exchange between equals. When we begin to look at the use of power in schools we may see that bullying behaviours can be seen in many interactions between pupils, parents, carers and teachers.

Who bullies whom?

Research identifies various characteristics of both bully and victim. Elliott (1991) writes,

"One study found that bullies were much more likely as adults to be violent, to have committed crimes, to have battered their children and to have difficulty with relationships with children who are not bullies."

Work from writers such as Lowenstein (1978), Stephenson and Smith (1987), Besag (1989), Woolfson (1989) and Olweus (1978) all describe features of bullies and victims. They tell us that boys bully both boys and girls whilst girls tend to bully only other girls. Boys are more likely to use physical aggression whilst girls are more likely to use verbal and psychological aggression. However, since there are exceptions these findings may be of interest but should not prevent us from making careful observations of actual behaviours in our own environments.

Much of the current literature identifies features that are common to victims, such as low self-esteem, co-ordination problems, poor hygiene, poor school achievement and are more likely to have problems at home. Again these stereotypes are of little practical use to us. If we have a particular model in our mind it may blinker us from seeing the less obvious types of bullying. Bullying can happen to anyone.

How common is it?

There is increasing research that attempts to quantify the size of the problem. We will argue that identifying the size of the problem is not particularly useful. Our interest was generated by the response of one girl who responded to bullying by taking an overdose of pills. Much of the research can be viewed with a critical eye on the basis of the size of the sample, the definitions being used, how the data is interpreted. What is clear from the research is that bullying does exist in British schools. It impinges on the lives of a sizable minority of pupils and it varies between schools.

Lowenstein (1978) suggests that 5% of boys between 11 - 16 are bullied. Newsom and Newsom (1984) found that 26% of mothers reported that their child had been bullied. Stephenson and Smith (1989) found that 23% of the pupils were either victims or bullies. Besag (1989) suggests that at least 10% of children in schools are probably, at some time involved as either bully or victim. Yates and Smith (1989) found in two comprehensive schools 10% of pupils reported that they were bullied once a week. Michelle Elliott conducted a study between 1984 - 1986 with 4000 children between the ages of 5 -16. She found that 68% complained of being bullied at some time, whilst 38% reported being bullied more than once and had experienced a particularly terrifying bullying incident. (Kidscape: Stop Bullying!) .

The tip of the iceberg?

It seems that many incidents are never reported. Most of the incidents occur whilst no adult is present, and there is a reluctance to 'tell tales'.

That bullying occurs in schools cannot be ignored as Maher (1990) writes, "Like child abuse, it is a problem which some teachers deny exists, but the evidence from both children and parents is that it affects the lives (and school achievement) of considerable numbers of children. On this basis alone it is a problem that schools should address, on which there should be a clearly defined policy and procedure."

Do we apply the term to one-off incidents of nastiness?

No - we would argue that one of the defining features of bullying is its persistence - that it involves misery making over a period of time or a 'reign of terror' which can frighten numbers of people who are on the fringe without necessarily experiencing the aggression.

Appendix two

what we see and hear

The former is restricted: it will often change when you are there. At best your observations may alert you to the likelihood that something is going wrong. If you are sensitive to the movement and body language of young people you may make your most accurate perceptions when you are some distance from a group and cannot hear what is being said.

what we are told

Telling tales

Many incidents of bullying are never reported. There is an unwritten rule amongst pupils that there is something wrong with 'grassing'. St. John Brooks (1985) reports on a "telling school" where the pupils are told that it is the bullies who invented the saying that you must not tell. The need for everyone in the school to recognise the damage that silence can cause is of crucial importance.

Questions we have been asked

You are not seen to be taking strong action - what will parents, carers, pupils, colleagues, think?

A school which has a clear, written policy on its anti-bullying procedures is not likely to incur disapproval from the community. In our experience most dissatisfaction arises when teachers do not take parental complaints seriously or when they respond by blaming the victim: - "It's six of one and half a dozen...", "She doesn't do much to help herself."

We have attended several parents meetings and explained the 'no blame approach' and the reaction has been very positive. Parents of victims may have feelings of revenge and anger but when we reassure them that something will be done we find they agree that the most important thing is to stop the bullying.

What do you do if there is a serious incident of violence?

When a pupil is seriously assaulted by another then the usual sanctions must be applied, even calling the police if appropriate. This does not mean that the 'no blame approach' cannot be tried as well since the particular incident of violence would not be discussed. The issue addressed is the misery of the victim and how that might be alleviated.

Surely you need to know exactly what went on?

It is only necessary to know that bullying is happening and to have the names of the young people involved. Any attempts to take accurate accounts about the events are likely to stir up further disputes, to increase hostility towards the victims and to waste a lot of time because the 'truth' may be hard to find and may vary from one person's perspective to another. Bullying is a complex process and you are not likely to discover all its ramifications and certainly not all its causes by questioning the participants.

What if only one bully is involved?

We believe that it is very rare that bullying takes place in real isolation - there is nearly always some knowledge and even consent from a group, even if they disapprove and refuse to join in. Secret bullying of one person by another is rare and hard to discover but if it is revealed then the 'no blame approach' might still be tried. A peer group could be given the opportunity to help put things right, even if they have not been involved in the unhappiness.

It might be worth considering whether interventions planned on child protection programmes could be helpful for these situations since they may apply to abuse of an individual by another who is not a member of the peer group.

What if the bully is seriously disturbed?

Pupils with seriously maladaptive behaviours should be helped in the usual way. The 'no blame approach' is planned to stop bullying, not to treat pathology. Any individual who is involved in this process may be offered other additional interventions or referred for specialist advice as necessary.

What about victims that provoke bullying? Why can't we help the victim directly?

Some victims may display behaviours which appear to encourage bullying from their peers. Any young person who has poor social and friendship skills or who is very unassertive should be offered help and support in order to learn appropriate social interaction. This should not be implied as a responsibility to stop the bullying for themselves.

When the group convenes to discuss the plight of the victim someone may suggest that he or she is encouraged to behave in a different way..."we could ask her to stop..." That is fine as long as the group take the responsibility to help her and the changes are within her ability.

Some reports from colleagues who have tried out the no blame approach.

Many of our colleagues have tried out the intervention and we have heard lots of encouraging reports of its success. A few are recorded below. There have been some slight modifications made to the plan, either because the approach was not explained carefully enough or because some changes seemed to suit the style of that teacher. For example, Julian Forsey took Paul in to meet with the group of bullies. This is fine if the victim is robust enough and willing to speak for himself.

Jean Gross - educational psychologist

On a visit to a comprehensive school I talked to a teacher who had been on a training course and tried out the 'no blame approach'. She had tried it with a group of three boys who had been picking on one particular lad, and later with a group of girls. She had found that the approach worked very well, and that the boys in particular had been very good at coming up with ideas about how to make things better.

She felt this was because, "I am calmer and observers who are not actually doing the bullying are involved. My initial feeling when someone has been bullied used to be to get the bully in and more or less say "Stop it!' Now it is more protracted...it might be the next day before I see the bully - but that actually helps."

Julian Forsey - primary school headteacher

The school of which I am the headteacher is situated in a 'leafy suburb' and has 230 pupils aged from four to eleven years. Barbara Maines had been recently transferred as the educational psychologist for the school. In conversation with her she mentioned that she had been doing some in-service work on dealing with bullying in schools, and I was very interested, as our playground seemed to be becoming a bit of jungle, with outbreaks of fighting and bullying taking place - not at all what we were used to!

I made detailed notes on what Barbara told me. At the next school staff meeting I mentioned the approach, and outlined what it entailed. My intention was that staff might consider trying it as a strategy, sort of adding it to their repertoire of ways of dealing with bullying. This was not to be! The staff pointed out that under that system there might be a whole host of anti-bullying initiatives going on side by side, without anyone else knowing what other people were doing. Staff felt that an 'anti bullying coordinator' was needed and that as I was the one who was suggesting it, then I should be that person - typical staff meeting jujitsu tactics!

The scene was set then, all we needed now was an incidence of bullying on which to try it out. I did not think that bullying was a big problem in the school, but then I don't have to survive long lunch hours on our playground so I'm not really the one to judge. (I am bullied by the staff, secretary and caretaker however - but that's another story).

Two weeks passed by and then the chance arose. Paul, a small, very gentle, considerate and sensitive boy in Y6 complained to his class teacher that the other boys were "calling him a girl." He had made the same complaint to one of the SMSAs, asking for any jobs which he could do in the school which would keep him from having to go out into the playground. The 'anti-bullying coordinator' swung into action!

I interviewed Paul on his own. I told him that I wanted to be able to tell the children who were name-calling just exactly what hurt they were causing. I elicited from him what precisely it was that the bullying group were saying and doing. I avoided asking for names, and played down any attempt at this stage to name or blame individuals. I asked him what he felt like when the other children were calling him names and carefully noted what he said. He said that he felt upset and that it made him want to cry. He wanted to be on his own. I asked him if it affected

29

him at home. He said that he sometimes couldn't sleep and that he lay awake worrying and crying. Often he didn't want to come to school. I noted all of this, and then explained to Paul that I wanted to convene a meeting. Those present would be him, me, the children who were name-calling, and any onlookers - those who were not actually involved but were often 'there or thereabouts' enjoying the spectacle. Paul agreed and we made a list of names.

The meeting took place that afternoon. About twelve children squeezed into my tiny room. I made the meeting as light as possible given the circumstances, emphasising that no-one was 'in trouble', rather that as a school community we had a problem. I explained that Paul was not enjoying life at school any more and continued by repeating all that Paul had told me - about the hurt which he was having to endure. Interjections from the group naming or blaming were played down with comments such as, "I don't really want to know any details like that, that's not what this meeting is for" etc. I kept on slipping in remarks to make it clear that this was a meeting, not a telling off.

After setting the scene I asked the big question; what can we do to stop Paul from feeling so bad? There was a whole babble of suggestions, all perfectly obvious ones on the theme of "we can stop calling him names." I dutifully wrote them down, saying what good ideas they were. I asked what we could do to make sure that everyone stuck to these ideas - remembered them - and was told that the members of the group would remind anyone who forgot. I thanked the group and said that we would meet again in a week's time to see how it was going.

Informal checks with Paul the next day revealed that it was going very well. One child - not a member of the group - had called him a girl though. I summoned this child to my room, and in the most unthreatening manner I could affect explained to him about the group, the problem, the meeting etc. and I invited him to join the review meeting in a few days time.

The review meeting at the end of the week was very short, but useful. I asked how it had gone and everyone said that it had been easy. Some claimed credit for 'suppressing' others. I played down any naming of names. I congratulated everyone involved, said that Paul was a much happier person as a result of their effort, thanked them and sent them on their way. I found the strategy quite difficult in terms of my own attitudes: Resisting the temptation to blame and tell-off bullies does not come easily! The children took it all in their stride and relationships were not damaged by the process - no recriminations were observed, as no-one had been 'got into trouble'. In terms of time expended the process was very economical - no more than an hour being spent on it in total. And yet the results have been quite staggering. There has been no recurrence of the problem whatsoever, and about six months have passed now. It seems to have been about the nearest thing possible to a 'Magic Aspirin' for bullying! All I need now is for another incident of bullying to occur so that I can try it again!

Jane Sleigh - comprehensive school teacher

Dealing with bullying the non-blameful way.

When using the non-blameful approach to bullying I have experienced a more positive response from the students. They are willing to be part of the 'support' group. I have usually asked the victim to give me names of friends as well as 'bullies and onlookers', so as to achieve a balance within the group. This releases the tension of all those present thinking, "What have I done?"

After explaining the victim's feelings I have frequently heard, "But it wasn't me" or "I didn't mean to!" This enables me to reinforce that the purpose of the meeting is not to apportion blame. The flushed faces and worried expressions then subside.

I have used various size 'support groups' ranging from one to half a class, depending on the nature of the situation.

The incident with one was a lad who had verbally abused another by calling him 'gay'. After speaking to both lads they agreed that I should explain to each how the other was feeling. The two then agreed to meet with me present. A civilised, mature discussion occurred and the lads left chatting amicably, having shaken hands and accepted apologies.

The half class group occurred because two girls were being teased about their religion and its beliefs. By calling the whole group I was able to explain the feelings of the girls and explain why their religion prevented them from joining in particular activities. The group took a long time to appreciate the concern of the two girls as lots of other undercurrents had also been occurring. Again, having established the non-blameful nature of the meeting we were able to continue more appropriately.

After the meeting one girl hung back and poured out why she had been so anxious. Explaining that she had always been accused of being the class bully and had hoped that the reputation had not followed her to Secondary school. I assured her that the information had not been passed onto the school. She left feeling reassured and happy about the way in which the matter had been dealt.

Pat Firth - comprehensive school deputy head

The 'no blame approach to bullying' at The Ridings High School.

The Ridings has always adopted a policy of bringing the 'victims' and 'bullies' together to try to resolve disputes but it wasn't until Pat Firth, the Deputy Head Liaison, went on the Maines/Robinson bullying course last November 1991 that the notion of involving colluders and observers was considered.

The 'No Blame' approach was discussed by the Senior Management Team and Year Heads and it was decided, with some reservations, to give it a go. Some staff felt parents would want punitive measures and others felt that sometimes punishment was necessary for the benefit of the school community as a whole. However all agreed to, at least, have a try.

Those Year Heads who have used the method have found that it works. e.g. Dick Hannaford, current Head of Year 10, had a young timid pupil called Jason (fictitious name) who was regularly bullied, i.e. picked on, called names, belittled and kicked by two Year 10 bullies. The Head of Year got the group together including observers (there were no colluders) to discuss Jason's feelings which were becoming so intense he was beginning to express an unwillingness to attend school. After two meetings, over a time period of two weeks, the bullies ceased, the victim was happy but subsequently the victim put sneezing powder in the observers sandwiches'. Again this was resolved.

Russ Hawkins, currently Head of Year 8, used the method several times to tease out issues, for example, 4 or 5 lads came to complain about 4 or 5 other boys who were making life unpleasant, e.g. name-calling, pushing, shoving whenever there was an opportunity. The Head of Year got all ten pupils together and they all expressed their feelings about what was happening. The Head of Year asked them what they thought should happen next? The victims wanted the bullying to cease and the perpetrators accepted that their behaviour was unfair. The strongest of the five bullies, in terms of personality, agreed that they should all back off. Upon checking the situation, in subsequent weeks, the intimidation had ceased totally. One boy who was part of the group has continued to bully totally different individuals and this has been dealt with using the same no blame approach. This also appears to have been successful.

Pat Firth, the Deputy Head, has used this approach to try and constitute a feeling of empathy after a bully had returned from a suspension. In this case the bully, a Year 11 girl, had severely attacked another in full public view outside the school gates; a real cat-fight ensued and a passer-by reported the incident.

Eventually the bully agreed she had been provoked, not by the victim, but by the colluders and observers. Her alleged friends had set her up; she felt more anger toward her mates than the victim. Subsequent meetings of all concerned seem to have solved the problem, as to date the violence has not recurred. This pupil, until this time, had a reputation for fighting both in school and in the community at large.

Each time the empathy method has been used it has worked, it takes time but no more so than collating individual statements from pupils. Also, we have had no parental come-back either in terms of positive or negative feedback. It would appear everyone just feels relieved!

Something that we have come to recognise more during the 'trial of this approach' is that the main protagonists are often the most intelligent pupils in the group and they can recognise the dynamics. The colluders and observers tend to be the less bright pupils who find it difficult to appreciate what is happening in group discussions. The power game is an interesting phenomenon which is not new but we hope by continuing to use this method we may eventually succeed in ameliorating the situation. The overall message about this approach is positive.

References

BESAG V. E.(1989) Bullies and Victims in Schools, Milton Keynes. O.U.P.

ELLIOTT M. (1990) *Kidscape, Stop Bullying*. Kidscape, World Trade Centre, Europe House, London. E1 9AA.

ELLIOTT M. ed. (1991) *Bullying - a practical guide to coping for schools*. Longman in association with Kidscape.

JONES E. (1991) *Practical considerations in dealing with bullying in secondary schools, in Bullying - a practical guide to coping for schools*. Longman in association with Kidscape, edited by Michelle Elliott.

LOWENSTEIN L.F. (1978) Who is the Bully. *Bulletin* British Psychological Society 31. pp147-149

MAHER P. (1990) Child Protection-Another View. *Pastoral Care*. September 1990 pp 9-12.

MAINES B. & ROBINSON G. (1991) *Stamp out Bullying*. Lucky Duck Publishin.

NEWSON J.& NEWSON E. (1984) *Parents Perspectives on Childrens Behaviour in Schools*, in Frude, N. & Gault H. Eds. Disruptive Behaviour in Schools. Chichester, Wiley.

OLWEUS D. (1978) *Aggression in the Schools: Bullies and Whipping-boys*. London, Wiley; Halsted Press.

PEARCE J. (1991) What can be done about the bully? in *Bullying - a practical guide to coping for schools*. Longman in association with Kidscape, edited by Michelle Elliott.

PIKAS A. (1989). The Common Concern Method for the Treatment of Mobbing. in Roland E & Munthe E. *Bullying, An International Perspective*. London, David Fulton.

ROBINSON G. & MAINES B. (1998) *Crying for Help. The No Blame Approach to Bullying*, Lucky Duck Publishing

ST. JOHN BROOKS (1985) The School Bullies. *New Society*, 6.12. 85. pp 363-365.

STEPHENSON P. and SMITH D. (1989) 'Bullying in the junior school', in D. P .Tattum and D. A. Lane, (eds), *Bullying in Schools*.

WOOLFSON R. (1989) Bullying at School. Part 2, The Bully and the Victim. *Health at School* Vol.4.6 pp 174-5.

YATES C. & SMITH P. (1989) Bullying in two English Comprehensive Schools, in Roland, E. & Munthe, E. *Bullying, An International Perspective*. London. David Fulton.

Extra copies of this workbook are available - Cost £4.00 each. It was prepared in 1992 at the start of our work on bullying in schools.

In 1998 we reviewed that work and published a book called Crying for Help which includes accounts of the recent research, an evaluation of the No Blame Approach, contributions from teachers, parents and victims.

Don't forget to visit our website for all our latest publications, news and reviews.

www.luckyduck.co.uk

New publications every year on our specialist topics:

- ▸ **Emotional Literacy**

- ▸ **Self-esteem**

- ▸ **Bullying**

- ▸ **Positive Behaviour Management**

- ▸ **Circle Time**

- ▸ **Anger Management**

- ▸ **Asperger's Syndrome**

- ▸ **Eating Disorders**

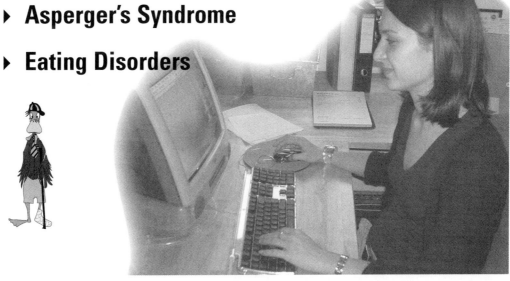